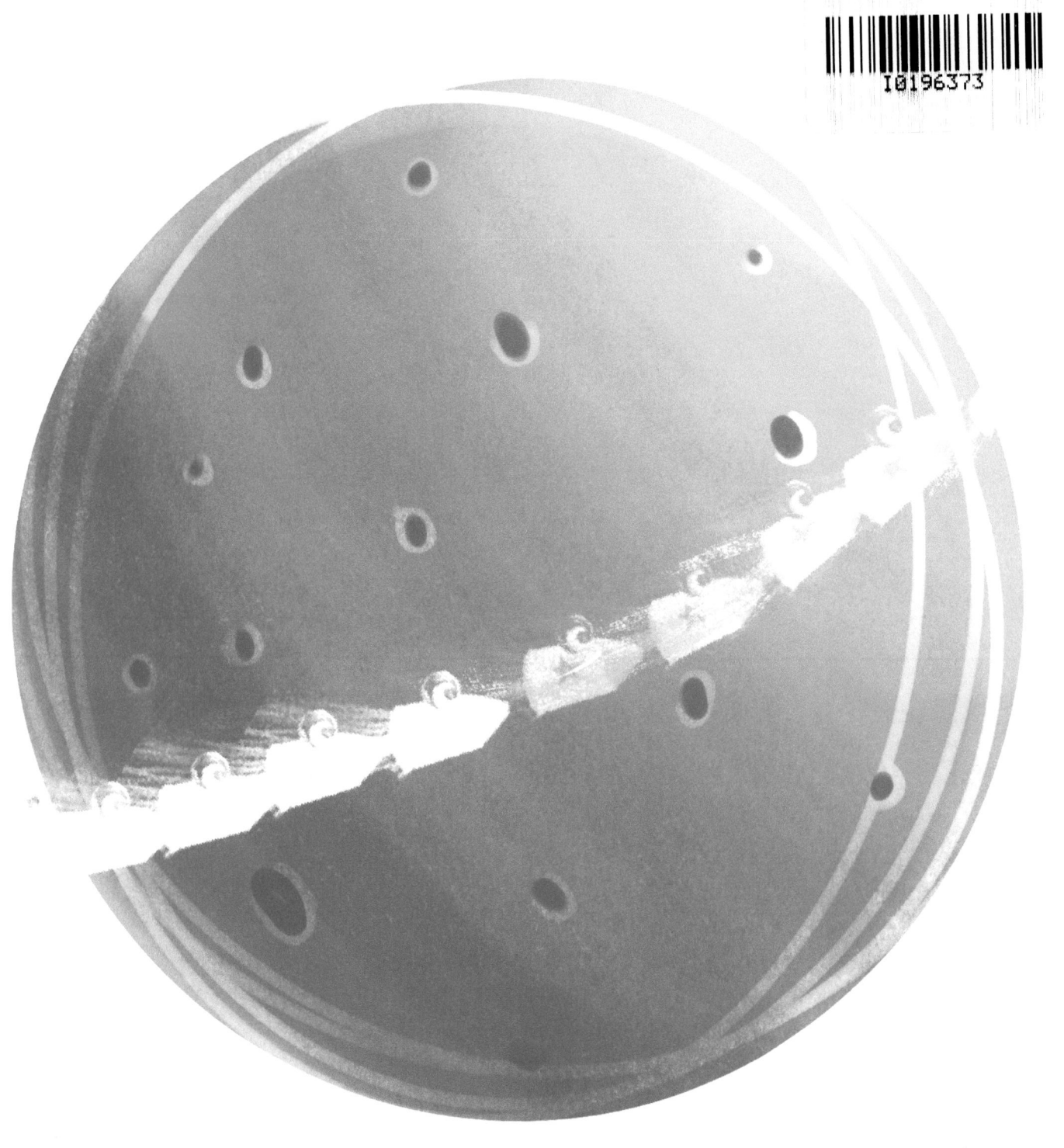

Copyright © 2023 Newzone Publishing

Written by: Alicia Hughes
Design and Illustrations by: Passant M. Ablal

All rights reserved. No part of this publication may be reproduced, distributed, or transmitted in any form or by any means, including photocopying, recording, or other electronic or mechanical methods, without the prior written permission of the publisher, except in the case of brief quotations embodied in critical reviews and certain other non-commercial uses permitted by copyright law.

ISBN: 978 1 3999 6970 3

Disclaimer:

The characters, story, and illustrations in this book are entirely fictional. Any resemblance to actual persons, living or dead, events, or locales is purely coincidental.

The information provided in this book is intended to educate and entertain young readers. It is not a substitute for professional medical or psychological advice. Parents and guardians are encouraged to discuss important topics covered in this book with their children and seek guidance from appropriate experts when necessary.

This book belongs to:

....

Teaching children about body boundaries is crucial for their development, confidence, and understanding of how they should be treated by others. When children know that they have the right to their own personal space, they gain ownership and the ability to make choices about their bodies. It's just as important for children to understand from a young age that they need to respect other people's body boundaries and ask for consent before entering their personal space.

This book explores these concepts in a child-friendly way, using familiar scenarios for children to discuss and engage with. It's important for both the reader and the child to take the time to understand each scenario and what it means to the characters involved. Through these discussions, children will learn about body boundaries, consent, and respect, which are important social skills that they will carry with them throughout their lives.

It's important for significant adults to model these behaviours for children, as this will have a lasting impact on their understanding of body boundaries and consent as they grow older.

Meet Stellar Scouts

Phoenix: Never leaves Zoom's side and he is a loyal well trained dog.

Zoom the brave Captain: Zoom is the leader of the space cadet crew. He's courageous, determined, and always ready for action.

Titan the strong Engineer: Titan is the muscle of the team. he's great at fixing things, building new gadgets, and keeping the ship running smoothly.

Luna the Navigator: Luna is responsible for keeping the space cadet ship on course. She's an expert at reading maps and finding her way through the cosmos.

Neutron the energetic pilot: Neutron loves to zoom around in the Space Cadet ship. She's got lightning-fast reflexes and can outmaneuver any obstacle.

Cosmo the curious Scientist: Cosmo is the brains of the operation. She's always asking questions, conducting experiments, and discovering new things about the universe.

Welcome to Stellar Scouts,
Where space adventures abound.
We find Captain Zoom having fun,
On the Captain's deck, jumping around.

But wait, who's this pushing and pulling?
It's Luna, and she wants the Captain's seat.
Zoom didn't like it, he jumped to his feet
He knew it was time for him to go, and that was it.

Zoom ran to the Captain's quarters,
Where his parents could be found.
He needed to talk to them right Away,
And get some comfort that
Was safe and sound.

Zoom's mom was quite the sight,
Her alien friend Samara was coming tonight,
Samara hugged and kissed with plenty to share,
Zoom felt quite uncomfortable, like he was in a snare.

He opened up to his parents and told them what's wrong,
About Luna's pushing
And how Samara's hugs lasted too long

"Zoom, dear Zoom, listen well" the dad said.
"Don't let anyone make you dwell.
Say no to touches that feel wrong,
And keep your body safe and strong."

His mom echoed, "Your body is special,
It's a treasure you should protect,
If someone makes you uncomfortable,
You have the power to object!"

"Our bodies are precious, this is true,
And our boundaries should be respected too.
Speak up with confidence and might,
Stand your ground, and shine your light
So listen up, it's time to know,
Invading space is a big no-no!"

"So come sit by me, let's talk about touch,
It's important to know, so let's not rush.
Your body belongs to you, that's the key,
Importantly, private parts are off-limits, you see,
So if someone touches you in a way that's not right,
Speak up and tell someone that you trust to make it alright

"Private parts belong to you, stay safe and sound in all you do.
Doctors may need to assess and inspect,
A child's health to find out if it's correct.
But always ensure a parent or guardian
Is near, to alleviate any concern or fear."

"It's vital for children to comprehend,
The contrast between a stranger and a friend,
And always be cautious of those they meet,
So they can stay safe and avoid deceit."

"Some people may offer rewards,
For inappropriate touch or play,
Children should avoid such situations,
And tell someone straight away."

"Trusted adults, like a guiding light,
Are there to help you, day or night.
If uncomfortable or unsafe, it's time to report,
To your trusted adults, for help and support."

"So, remember what I've said little Zoom,
If you feel unsafe, don't be misled.
Speak up, ask for help, and shout,
And follow your parents' advice, without a doubt."

"Don't be afraid to say to Samara,
I don't want a hug today.
It's your body, your voice.
So instead of hugs, a high five can be your choice."

With his mom's guidance, Zoom felt empowered and free,
To express his feelings and be the best that he can be.
And instead of hugs and kisses, he gave a high five.
He felt proud and empowered,
And knew he was safe to thrive.

And now we come to the end of the tale, With five messages, so you won't fail!

If something doesn't feel right or makes you feel uncomfortable, you should tell someone you trust like your mom, dad, or teacher.

You can choose how you want to say hello or goodbye to someone, and it's okay to give a high five instead of a hug or kiss if that's what you prefer.

There are parts of your body that are private, and should only be seen or touched by you or a doctor, when your mom or dad is with you.

It's important to be careful around people you don't know, and not to go with anyone you don't recognize, even if they seem nice.

Your body is special, and it belongs to you. You have the right to say no to any touch that doesn't feel right or makes you uncomfortable.

www.ingramcontent.com/pod-product-compliance
Lightning Source LLC
Chambersburg PA
CBHW042131040426
42450CB00003B/147